Zen Duende

Collaborative Poems by

Eric Greinke
&
Glenna Luschei

Also by Eric Greinke (partial listing)

Sand & Other Poems
Caged Angels
The Last Ballet
Iron Rose
Masterpiece Theater (with Brian Adam)
The Broken Lock (Selected Poems 1960-1975)
The Drunken Boat & Other Poems From The French Of Arthur Rimbaud
Selected Poems 1972-2005
Up North (with Harry Smith)
Wild Strawberries
Catching The Light - 12 Haiku Sequences (with John Elsberg)
Traveling Music
The Potential Of Poetry
Beyond Our Control (with Hugh Fox)
Conversation Pieces - Selected Interviews
All This Dark - 24 Tanka Sequences (with John Elsberg)
For The Living Dead - New & Selected Poems
Poets In Review

Also by Glenna Luschei (partial listing)

Letter To The North
Redwoods
Unexpected Grace
Driving Through Light
Farewell To Winter
Bare Root Season
Matriarch
Cassandra Speaks Up
Spirit Of Place
Cities Of Cibola And Other Poems
Pianos Around The Cape
Shot With Eros
Libido Dreams
Total Immersion
Salt Lick: A Retrospective of Poetry
Witch Dance - Selected Poems
Leaving It All Behind
The Sky Is Shooting Blue Arrows

Zen Duende

Collaborative Poems by

Eric Greinke
&
Glenna Luschei

PRESA PRESS
Rockford, MI

Acknowledgments
The following poems have been published or are forthcoming in:
First Literary Review -East – *The Show* & *Silk Road*
Forge -- *Lone Bones*
Ibbetson Street – *Hugh*

Cover art by Anna Wylie.
Photograph of Glenna Luschei by Phil Taggart.
Photograph of Eric Greinke by Anna Wylie.

With special thanks to: Brian Landis for heeding Glenna's call to Bodhisattvahood, & to Cindy Hochman, Tim McLafferty & Doug Holder.

To the memory of Hugh Fox & Harry Smith.

First Edition

Printed in the United States of America

ISBN: 978-0-9965026-1-0

Library of Congress Control Number: 2015949803

PRESA PRESS
PO Box 792 Rockford MI 49341
presapress@aol.com www.presapress.com

Contents

"Moment after moment, everyone comes out from nothingness. This is the true joy of life."
– D. T. Suzuki

"I heard an old maestro *of the guitar say: 'The* duende *is not in the throat: the* duende *surges up, inside, from the soles of the feet."*
– Federico Garcia Lorca

"That *the world is, is the mystical.*
– Ludwig Wittgenstein

1

Life Is

spirit finding its way home

a fire in the hole

spinning out of control

the spatter of rain

orange clouds in the evening

a tree of microbes

hiding in plain sight

an angel dancing on the head of a pin

pewter in the tavern

a merganser consuming fish

waking to another day

music of the wind

a slow turtle crossing a busy highway

dirt on the mat

blue sky in winter

billions of planets in love

a lake filling up after drought

here & not here

a whirlpool of swirling souls

a sparrow huddling in a snowy hedge

a bird of prey zooming in on the sparrow

a storm heading toward shore

an algae-covered pond

young men killed in battle

a fresh egg

a vulture eating roadkill

a condemned man eating his last meal

rushing to meet the deadline

the uncarved block

a snowflake

red sky in the morning

waiting, waiting

a promiscuous tornado

a Spring breeze

pollen in the wind

a seagull floating miles from shore

a set of footprints outside the window

menace lurking under the bliss

dancing the Hokie Pokie

a vapor trail on a blue sky

an eagle flying over open water

a slow thaw

polar bears running out of ice

wind over a graveyard

forever arriving

an orphan scrounging for food

a ewe waiting for shearing

a battle about to begin

coming out of the closet

the tea ceremony

a runaway train

a ship on the bottom of the ocean floor

old women who go on alone

a hummingbird crossing the Gulf of Mexico

a plume of smoke

a cold wind in March

going nowhere

carnivorous

an interconnected waterway

a surprise snow late in the season

the ones who went before

a hot breakfast on a cold morning

glass of wine at day's end

forgetting what time it is

a fight coming out of nowhere

a late snow on spring crocuses

germinating rain

a sparkle in a dog's eye

a song you can't get out of your head

hair salty from the ocean

the crackling of a campfire

a teenage car crash going to the prom

parents who can't afford to feed their children

a question that is never answered

a good sleep after a long walk

an avalanche

dancing on the edge of a chasm

a lock with no key

an endless feast

a beam of sunlight through dark clouds

an early crocus breaking through the snow

a murder of crows

betrayal from where you least expect it

the fiery heart of the planet

a hard road to travel

glow of silver in the dark

ticket on the way to a funeral

dark dance of the scorpion

a hole in the fire

flying at the speed of light

2

Time and the Dream

We are at one with the other stars
especially the ones about to explode.
I am not ready to say goodbye to this glittering life.
I am burning hotter than ever,
a lotus arising from filthy waters
opening my petals to the sun.
Let all the bees come here for nectar.
Let all the locks open to my keys.
It is time at last for us to enter the forbidden room
where the eternal amaranth still blooms.
It is time for us to hold hands, imbibe the drug.
It is time for warm blood to flow between us.
When we awake it will be on another planet.
There we'll breathe the air of dreams.

Silk Road

The Silk Road to the future is around the corner.
The map is imprinted on our palms.
The stream is imprinted on our lifelines
And flows inevitably into the ocean of love.

The Silk Road of the past is gone forever.
The sap floods from amputated branches.
After we row through the waters of regret,
The misty shore appears, like the day we met.

Ghost

He reached for the flashlight and it was handed to
him.
He hadn't noticed the stranger in the darkness.
A chill ran through him as he thought it might be a
ghost
Or a memory that became a shadow.
After all this time could they return to haunt him?
The big explosion seemed like only yesterday!
His other arm was still paralyzed.
Why, then, was he waving it wildly?
Could they have returned to remove the curse?
What body part would they want in return?
Instinctively he put his palm over the ruby in his
eye.
When he found it already gone, he panicked.
He wondered if they planned to dismember him.
They hadn't done that for several centuries!
Perhaps it was time for him to move on.
If he hurried, he might yet catch his brain.

Connection

The fire broke out while they were gone.
It wasn't the house, but their love-life.
"We're just like young kids," they said.
It was the romantic allure of the island.
It was the music they heard in their heads.
They were down on the bony ground.
Feeling the tide inching up their legs, they
Stood together in a flood of joy.

Bones

In the know, in the now,
I am ready to implode.
So I go around this town alone.
At the Festival I look for a buddy.
I found a clown whose name was Eddie.
I am his. He is mine already.
Someday we hope to take it on the road.
Two mimes in tune with time.
Loaded down with all we've ever known.

In the know, in the now,
I keep my soul inside a stone.
Oh Eddie, can you help me outta here?
My heart is steady, but I'm not ready.
I have to learn to go ahead, my hand in his.
Instead I burn, my feet aflame.
I kick my way around this town.
I fling my lonely bones into the ditch.
Eddie said, "They'll make us rich."

Exposure

The morning grass is wet with dew.
We take our old bones out to walk
A path that winds between lilacs.

How fragrant the lilacs after winter.
We bring our old bones home,
dry out our socks before the fire

and watch the dying embers flare
like small sunbursts, then sputter
into orange horizons I remember

when we were young
and had our gang around us.
Are we able I wonder to carry

that spirit to the end
before our last spark
dissipates into infinity?

Yes! All it takes is memory
and will to take these bones out
again into the wet morning grass.

The Show

The swans applauded the sky with their wings.
The clouds lifted and took a bow while
The sun felt secretly proud.

Trout

I was fishing for steelhead on the Rogue,
my autumn pilgrimage, when I remembered
how you cast your line out, over fluid space,
praying to find what lies beneath.
Then, the green depth revealed a surprise.
In all my years on the Rogue, I had never
encountered
a trout that looked at me with human eyes.
What could this creature be? Someone/thing
I imagined, or never noticed before?
Suddenly my line jerked and I nearly lost
my balance as those eyes dived back down.
I knew I had no choice. It was now
a matter of conscience, so I quickly
entered the waters and met my doom

Cartoon

I woke this morning from a dream.
I went to Germany to see a doctor and it was
    freezing.
He said I was changing into a giant condor.
He took the x-rays to prove it but
when I looked, all I saw was a Looney Toon.
Could it be true? Was it so many years
since I first saw Bugs Bunny in the mirror?

Return

I fell asleep beneath an oak
and had a dream that made me
know we met here years ago.
What happened? You promised
that I'd never wake alone
but here I am, and you are gone.
Do we find true love but in dreams?
That's your one return it seems.

The Promise

What promise the first cool days of May bring
Leaves are grasshoppers in first spring.

Though spring rains soak us
They bring up the crocus.

While we run for cover
we still pray these days go on forever.

In time we flow together
Into another river.

Lone Bones

1. THE GREAT MISTAKE
   Everyone I knew liked to submit poems there.

2. "ENERGY IS ETERNAL DELIGHT" (Blake)
   No one knew the rock was hollow.

3. REMINDER
   The pines whispered secrets all night.

4. CLOSING TIME
   Thoughts of you bring smiles to me.

5. EXTREME SPORTS
   You may owe a late enrollment penalty.

6. A SIMPLE WISH
   Could you please email me directions?

7. THE RUMOR
   Cyclers and surfers are welcome on board with
   bikes and boards.

8. THE MAIN ARGUMENT
   Big trout suspend in pools of love.

9. THE DEAD PART
   Everyone at the premiere knew it was bad.

10 FASHION RACE IN LAS VEGAS
The transformation was immediate.

11. IN THE THICK OF IT
Seven swans staked a territory.

12. BRICKS SINKING IN DEEP WATER
I had my hands to myself.

13. CHAPTER TWO
We loved the clairvoyant moonlight.

14. LIVES IN LIMBO
The apple cider had fermented.

15. VIVE LA FRANCE
Swords were integral to the decor.

16. TABLES FOR TWO
The road was littered with rocks.

17. SPECIAL INVITATION
A red-tailed hawk wheeled above us.

18. PREDESTINATION
We sidestepped some people who were selling
tour-bus tickets.

19. SAD CAFE
I miss Hugh more than I ever thought possible.

20. MAZE OF LOVE
I hear myself speaking to my grandchildren as
my grandmother spoke to me.

21. PRENUPTIAL
It would be great if that artist died in his studio.

22. BAD DREAM
As a preferred client, your tax return
appointment has been given priority.

23. STANDARD FARE
As soon as your read her fiction, Ferrante's
restraint seems wisely self protective.

24. IMPLOSION
As typing increasingly eclipses handwriting,
will our humanity disappear?

25. VICTORY
This is a smoke-free facility.

26. THE ROCKIES
We knew them at their peak.

27. THE DRAW
We have outlived all of them.

28. EACH PAGE A WORK OF ART
Every pencil in the drawer was dull.

29. ONCE UPON A TIME
Our tryst was filtered by a champagne dawn.

30. MAMA MIA!
All it needed was a little salt.

31. CREATE A TRANQUIL SANCTUARY
The creek water was clear & cold.

32. MAN AND MACHINE
They sold the farm & retired to town.

33. CLIFFHANGERS
The earthquake was inconvenient.

34. HEAVEN IS FOR REAL
She dreamed of snow-capped cedars.

35. A VISIT TO COLUMBUS CIRCLE
All we knew was meadow.

36. CLOWN MUSEUM
The cat's eyes were the only source of light.

37. OLD BONES
At last the tie was broken.

38. DIEHARD
Gamers Eric and Glenna strive for that epic win.

39. BIG FUN
All day I've been watching the coneflowers.

40. JIMMY THE GREEK
He dropped anchor like a pro.

41. ALL WE KNEW
Jacaranda petals blanket a narrow stretch of highway.

42. LOST HORIZONS
You know how sometimes our bodies aren't ours.

43. WEIGHT OF TIME
Shelves in my kitchen bear antique rose cups.

44. MIDLIFE CRISIS
I am a foreigner here.

45. THE SAD TRUTH
In a dream muddy water is a sign of death.

46. WHAT KIND OF FOOL AM I?
Avoid burial in a storm.

47. NOSTALGIA FOR THE INFINITE
Where blue songs warm the shallows.

48. INTO THE SILENCE
Polar wind penetrated my chest.

49. THE STORY OF A FATHER
The inevitable set-up was underway.

50. THE NEW BOOM IN CELEBRITY PHILANTHROPY
It was the longest nightmare ever.

51. LOOKING GOOD
Laughter bubbled over the rapids.

52. ROYAL FLUSH
There was no exit, no escape.

53. PEACE OF MIND
The canyons were filled with flowers.

54. THE MAN WITHOUT A FACE
I couldn't turn away.

55. CULTURAL TREASURE
Her rose tattoo said it all.

56. COMPLIMENTARY MASSAGE
It was all an elaborate ritual.

57. WHAT DID WE TELL YOU?
The love child was out of control.

58. SUPPLY LINE
We gratefully acknowledge our sponsors.

59. BORROWED GLORY
Ossian was still regarded as the Celtic Homer.

60. THE IMPOSSIBLE DREAM
Never doubt that a small group of thoughtful, committed citizens can change the world. (Margaret Mead).

61. LOST LOVE
The group stood at 26 members.

62. THE DISTANT SHORE
For me, the motif is the starting point, not the end.

63. MARGIN CALL
Still, she'd rather be shot.

64. ZOO CHILD
Beansie is the third bear to have escaped.

65. SANITY CLAUSE
I can't do it.

66. INSPIRATION
I reach into the bag and pull out an old revolver.

67. THE FINAL COUNTDOWN
If you have no god, make some.

68. BREAKAPART
When he was with her, he became a ghost.

69. HOLDING THE SHOULDER
We were still twenty miles from Boston!

70. PLENTY OF MEAT
It was the birth of a movement.

71. HAWKS OF FATE
Rats ruined the arrangements.

72. EXIT THE PROFESSOR
He loved her like a name brand.

73. WARNED
What reasonable person could refuse?

74. CARGO
Inside the egg was a tiny suitcase.

75. RECOMMENDED FOR DAILY USE
They were all donut crazy.

76. A STEP BACK IN TIME
The peonies and asters formed a band.

77. THE MUMMY'S GHOST
Only the brave will ever know.

78. SUMMER DREAM
I loved the snow flurries.

79. EMOTIONAL REQUIREMENT
Kindly proceed to the front desk for packaging supplies.

80. DARKNESS AT NOON
Don't forget the time change!

81. SEIZE THE CARP
There's never a better time.

82. POLITICS AS USUAL
Suite rates are per night, plus tax.

83. LOVE MONKEYS
But we needed the eggs.

84. THE GESTURE
I have requested delivery.

85. THE DUH FACTOR
We are both of legal drinking age.

86. PLENTY OF NOTHING
There's nothing like Maine lobster.

87. UNIVERSAL TRUTH
We must hold to what we cherish.

88. OH BOY
The sun shouted joy.

89. DRINKING ON SUNDAY
Strangers lack the intimate touch.

90. THE IMPOSSIBLE RHYME
He saw time wind into a bind.

91. AN EDUCATION
An emerald beetle glistened briefly.

92. MORE OF THE SAME
The pines whispered new rumors.

93. SPEED OF LIGHT
Even the dock shook in the quake.

94. ATTENTION TO DETAIL
Carbohydrates defeated Napoleon.

95. ONION BREATH
The spies were excited by the odor.

96. SOMEONE MISSING OUT
It was the only love triangle in their circle.

97. GOT A LIGHT?
Wax dripped from the sky all day.

98. GRECIAN FORMULA
Samson's haircut was the worst.

99. THE WINNER
A tiny sparrow brought the news.

100. COAL MINES
The whole country was a mental suburb.

4

Hugh

Hugh loved the complexity of the world.
When I told Hugh I loved him unconditionally,
he wept.
As a child, Hugh was a prodigy on the piano.
Hugh's mother raised him as a girl teaching him
about linen and fine china.
She wanted Hugh to become a doctor, but Hugh
was drawn to the arts.
Hugh turned out a doctor of the soul and the heart.
When Hugh couldn't consummate his marriage,
he wrote and published a funny novel about it.
Like all of our gang, Hugh treated sorrow with
humor.
Hugh was fluent in several languages.
The languages Hugh couldn't speak, he just
made up.
Educated by Jesuits, Hugh became a Jew.
When he visited me, Hugh bowed his head
to a Christian blessing.
Hugh once had on such heavy eye make-up
that we asked if he'd been mugged.
Women were envious of Hugh 's pretty dresses.
In his last years, Hugh went back to wearing his
little gray hat.
In his last days, Hugh called his friends every night.
Hugh had beautiful blue ice eyes.
After his face lift in Brazil, Hugh looked
much younger.
For a decade, Hugh fought the cancer that
killed him.

Because of his jocular nature friends could no
believe Hugh was dying.
For Hugh, it was both real and unreal.
Hugh never made it to his eightieth but there was
a cake for him at his grave.
Hugh loved a wide variety of ethnic foods.
Strange Hugh always ate melon for supper
at home.
The walls of Hugh's home were decorated with
tribal masks.
Much as Hugh adored the exotic, his favorite city
was Chicago.
Hugh traveled to South and Central America
every year.
People took Hugh for a native Spaniard or
Brazilian.
Hugh took people for who they were.
Hugh was a populist par excellence.
Hugh had a special kind of courage.
Hugh also stood up for the underdog and his
beloved friends.
Hugh was an enigmatic figure in American
literature.
Critics sometimes tried to place Hugh as a beatnik.
Many of Hugh's best poems were written under
the name of Connie.
Hugh loved women and they adored him.
Hugh married three times and maintained
active, friendly relationships with his ex-wives.
Hugh's third wife bought his second wife a
new house.
One wall in Hugh's bedroom had floor to ceiling
bookshelves of his published work.
When he visited friends, he looked for the

Hugh Fox section on their bookcases.
Hugh wrote poetry, fiction, drama and non-fiction.
Hugh's treatise on Peruvian archeology may have
bordered on science fiction.
However, Hugh's works of fiction were really true.
Hugh was the elephant in every room.
Hugh was the Cheshire Cat on every branch.
Hugh was the needle in every heart.
Hugh stomped the terra like a giant.
Sometimes Hugh strode on high heels.
Once people accepted Hugh as Connie,
Hugh went back to being Hugh.
A relief because Connie's bear hugs were
even more back wrenching than Hugh's.
Hugh was plagued by wildly surreal dreams.
When Hugh approached various strangers in
various languages, one never knew what
to expect.
Hugh hated barriers between people.
Hugh was an enormous friendly sheep dog
who bounded up to people.
Hugh was a chameleon.
It made Hugh sad when he was not the darling.
Hugh didn't get enough approval from his parents.
Hugh got plenty of approval from us, although at
times he shocked us.
Hugh needed intense relationships.
Whenever Hugh made a statement he expected a
dialogue or confrontation.
Hugh's death was a shock, because Hugh was
so alive.
He was the end of a Millennium.
Hugh called it 'The Invisible Generation.'
No one could call Hugh invisible.

Hugh called his magazine *Ghost Dance.*
Hugh was crazy about the Mimeo Revolution.
Hugh reviewed over a thousand books over a
forty year period.
Everyone wanted to score a review by Hugh.
Although he was a Professor of Modern Languages,
Hugh liked to use nouns as verbs.
But when Hugh windowed his verbs, people could
see right through them.
Hugh liked to open The Doors of Perception.
Revelation was everything to Hugh.
Everything was a revelation to Hugh.
Hugh got to places right on time.
Sometimes Hugh upset people with his candor.
Like it or not, Hugh always spoke the truth.
Hugh was huge.
Hugh's manner was delicate yet robust.
Hugh could be Quixotic.
Hugh was at his zenith aiding a damsel in distress.
Histrionic Hugh.
Honorable Hugh.
Hurricane Hugh.
Hugh Horribilus.
Harlequin Hugh.
A huge huzzah for Hugh!
Hail to Hugh, the Heffable Horralump!
Hozanna to Hugh in the Highest.
Hugh! Hugh! Hugh! Hugh! Hugh.

Harry

Harry Smith loved to play the ponies.
Harry was like a big, friendly growly bear.
Harry was prodigiously generous and people
called him "Daddy Bucks."
Harry was expelled from Brown University
for declaring his dormitory independent.
Harry played fisticuffs with his grandmother.
Harry was a great literary activist.
With a group of friends, Harry founded the first
independent publishers' committee, COSMEP.
Harry loved to smoke, but it killed him.
Harry had an embolism once but he lived many
years after that.
Harry owned a small island in Maine.
Harry had an impressive art collection in his home
at Brooklyn Heights.
Harry had a big warehouse full of books
he published.
Harry had everything, even a dog named
Christopher.
Harry's self-indulgence was matched only by his
extreme generosity.
People stopped Harry in Brooklyn streets not
only to ask for money but also for his opinion
and advice.
Harry often used his influence to help others.
In spite of his great generosity, Harry expected
friends to take turns picking up the check.
Harry was complicated.
Harry had a way of speaking in stumbling

sentences so people never knew the power
of his ideas until the end of his discourse.
Harry put the 'general' in 'generalist.'
The name of Harry's magazine *The Smith*
contained a riddle.
Harry loved to work in his garden.
Sometimes Harry brought Hugh Fox to New York
to help with his magazine.
Hugh had his own room at Harry's house.
Harry and Hugh were alike in a hefty build but
were opposite natures.
Harry's greatest talent was recognizing talent
in others.
Harry's second greatest talent was in nourishing
and funding the talents he recognized.
Harry's poems and essays were declarative
personal statements.
Harry loved Fitzgerald's notion that you were a
genius if you could hold two opposing points of
view without cracking up.
Harry loved his double-ended surfboat.
Harry enjoyed all water activities, especially
steel-head fishing.
With his captain's beard and bulk, Harry could've
been cast as Ahab.
Harry could have been cast as the great
white whale.
Harry could have been cast as Falstaff.
Harry published a book by his great mentor,
Menke Katz.
Harry and Menke published two collaborative
poetry collections called *Two Friends* and
(tongue in cheek) *Two Friends II*.
Birch Brook Press published Harry's book, "The

Sexy Sixties."
Harry's last book, *Little Things*, was published by Presa Press.
In his last years, Harry married his great love, an Irish dancer.
In his last years, Harry quit publishing and moved to Maine.
In his last years, Harry gave his personal archives and small press editions to friends as Xmas gifts.
Harry's barn in Maine was full of books that he published that didn't sell.
Barns and houses full of books and furniture, Harry still adored attending antique auctions at great estates.
Harry wanted to revive the epic poem.
Though Harry was an Easterner, he thought the explorations of Lewis & Clark would make a swell epic poem.
Harry's best epic poem was *Trinity 9/11*.
Harry could have written an epic poem about Ferdinand the Bull.
In the last weeks of his life, Harry worked on his last book.
Harry just didn't have time to die.
Harry died at the age of 76.
A favorite memory of Harry: leaning back at table smoking and philosophizing.
Harry thought MFA programs were destructive to literature.
Harry deplored the conventional, feared that the alternative presses were becoming too much like the commercial ones.
Harry valued originality above all.

Harry valued humor second.
Harry said that a Great Poet should be a
    Neanderthal.
ET would have made a fabulous poet according
    to Harry.
Harry was an iconoclast.
Now he's an icon.

5

Zen Duende

ERIC: In your poetry, the quality that stands out the most for me is the expansive, transcendental spirituality that lies just below the surface of your poems, what the South Americans call 'duende.' Does this quality come from your exposure to South American poetry?

GLENNA: I feel that my very muse is duende, the sense that the soul comes to life when death is near. Many of my poems are light hearted, my way of taunting death, a very dangerous practice since a misstep could be fatal. I don't like Spanish bull fighting but I understand and appreciate the ritual of the dance of death.

Federico Garcia Lorca who wrote best of the duende said that death was the national Spanish past time. I realize that I court disaster and death. I like the work with the hidden in poetry, to preserve the hermetic quality in my work. It is the quality I keep most hidden but here you have gone and outed me. I think I was drawn to Spanish poetry because of the duende and Spanish poetry probably has increased the inclination which brought me to it in the first place.

E: Recognition of the transcendental potential of poetry is usually realized early in life, if it happens at all. I can understand your phrase "the inclination that brought me to it in the first place," in that context. When did you first realize that poetry could help expand awareness? Was death a part of that first realization?

G: I don't remember a death early in my life but my family spoke of death on a daily basis not in a frightening way, but more like the Day of the Dead in Mexico, a curiosity and a communion.

I think I have always felt poetry was awareness. At ten or so I asked my friend whose father owned a slaughter house if I could go with her to see an animal killed. I got up early and met her at the butcher shop. It happened so fast. The steer ran into the room, my friend's father shot him and then the men quickly hosed off the cement. The reason I entreated my friend to let me see this was because I wanted to be a writer and I needed this experience. As a young person, I also wanted to see an autopsy but I never have.

My family spoke of death and of those who had gone before every day. My grandparents loved to visit coffin factories, the inside padding as luxuriant as bridal dresses. We talked of coffins with bells inside of them so a person could ring if he was accidently buried. I adored the stories of Edgar Allen Poe about people who had been falsely buried. I knew all the werewolf and vampire mythologies.

My grandparents drove us to the cemetery nights after supper where we knew the markers by name and took offerings to the grave marked "kitty." We danced on Johnny Shoemaker's grave. One of my brothers' friends still writes about the time he begged to stay all night at our house because our ghost stories frightened him so much he was afraid to walk home.

E: You mention Lorca in regard to duende. Was he also a main influence on your writing style? What about Octavio Paz, whom I love for his transcendentalism? What do you think about Neruda?

G: Federico is my mentor because he is a mystery. On one of the covers of *Café Solo* I quoted his "El misterioso nos da la vida." He is translatable but still impenetrable. For instance his "verde. Que te quiero verde." It appears his lover is a green tree but how would we know?

I have studied with Paz and crossed paths with Neruda. As a student in Chile I was too shy to approach Neruda. I think the reason I light up for the Latinos is because their warmth brings me out of my reserved Iowa nature into my essence.

E: Catching on to ones own blessing is essential Transcendentalism. It's well-known that Neruda was a big disciple of Whitman.

I notice other international influences in your poetry. Did ancient Chinese poetry also help you discover your own voice in the way that Lorca did?

G: Right now Chinese poetry is a predominate influence in my life, the idea of Lao Tsu's uncarved block as a model for the poem and the poet. I am studying Buddhism and trying to work with acceptance and loss, letting go.

I have been trying very hard to separate essence from attribute and in expressing myself as I really am. At the same time. I am trying to forget myself.

E: Zen Buddhism helps one achieve a state which is really duende under another name. It's the state of mind that matters, not what we call it. The Buddha said "Those who decide 'I will die' stop being afraid. How could they fear even the visions of death?" Are the Zen poets and the Hispanic duende poets really mining the same territory? As we age, do we peel layers off our onion to get to the essence?

G: Your question about duende and Zen is intriguing. In duende we count on death to bring us closer to art, to poetry, to make us feel more alive. Duende makes the hair on our arms stand up. Is not fear and excitement part of the duende?

In Zen we know that life and death is the same thing and there is no fear. But mining the same field, yes.

E: Basically, I think the expansion of the ego toward oceanic oneness is what Zen and duende have in common. In Zen we empty ourselves of expectations and material concerns to perceive more fully the oneness of nature. In duende the ego also expands through emptying.

Many people believe that Zen is the emptying

of the ego, but it isn't that simple. We empty the ego of the disparate (like fear) and personal, but *expand it* in the direction of the universal simultaneously. So, it's letting the world fill us up. The Buddha said "Of all mindfulness meditations, that on death is supreme."

Author's Bios

Eric Greinke's work has appeared in the *California Quarterly, The Delaware Poetry Review, Gargoyle, Ginyu* (Japan), *The Green Door* (Belgium), *The Journal* (UK), the *New York Quarterly*, the *Paterson Literary Review, The Pedestal Magazine, Poem, Prosopisia* (India), *The South Carolina Review, The University of Tampa Review* and many others. He is one of twenty American poets included in the new international anthology *The Second Genesis: An Anthology of Contemporary World Poetry* (Anuraag Sharma, Ed.; ARAWLII Press, Ajmer, India, 2014). His most recent book is *For The Living Dead - New & Selected Poems* (Presa Press, 2014).

Glenna Luschei's poems have appeared in *The American Poetry Review*, *Beloit Poetry Journal*, *The Chiron Review*, *Fox Chase Review*, *Patterson Literary Review*, *Pembroke*, *Ploughshares*, *Prairie Schooner* and many other journals. Her most recent book is *The Sky Is Shooting Blue Arrows* (University of New Mexico Press, 2014). She is one of twenty American poets included in the new international anthology *The Second Genesis: An Anthology of Contemporary World Poetry* (Anuraag Sharma, Ed.; ARAWLII Press, Ajmer, India, 2014). She is former Poet Laureate of San Luis Obispo, California.

Selected Presa Press Titles

John Amen
At The Threshold Of Alchemy
Guy Beining
Nozzle 1-36
Louis E. Bourgeois
Alice
Kirby Congdon
Selected Poems & Prose Poems
Athletes
Kirby Congdon - Sixty-five Years of Poetry
Remarks And Reflections - Essays
Hugh Fox
Blood Cocoon - Selected Poems Of Connie Fox
Time & Other Poems
Eric Greinke
The Potential Of Poetry
Conversation Pieces - Selected Interviews
For The Living Dead - New & Selected Poems
Poets In Review
Ruth Moon Kempher
Retrievals
Kerry Shawn Keys
The Burning Mirror
Book Of Beasts
Transporting, A Cloak Of Rhapsodies
Night Flight
Arthur Winfield Knight
High County
Champagne Dawns
Richard Kostelanetz
PO/EMS
More Fulcra Poems
Purling Sonnets
Linda Lerner
Living In Dangerous Times
Donald Lev
Only Wings - 20 Poems Of Devotion
Where I Sit

Lyn Lifshin
In Mirrors
Lost Horses
Glenna Luschei
Seedpods
Total Immersion
Witch Dance - New & Selected Poems
Sprouts
Leaving It All Behind
Gerald Locklin
From A Male Perspective
Deep Meanings - Selected Poems 2008-2013
Peter Ludwin
Rumors Of Fallible Gods
Gary Metras
The Moon In The Pool
Stanley Nelson
Pre-Socratic Points & Other New Poems
Limbos For Amplified Harpsichord
City Of The Sun
B. Z. Niditch
Captive Cities
Roseanne Ritzema
Inside The Outside - An Anthology Of Avant-Garde American Poets
(includes: Kirby Congdon, Doug Holder, Hugh Fox, Eric Greinke, John Keene, Richard Kostelanetz, Lyn Lifshin, Richard Morris, Stanley Nelson, Lynne Savitt, Mark Sonnenfeld, Harry Smith, and A. D. Winans)
Lynne Savitt
The Deployment Of Love In Pineapple Twilight
Steven Sher
Grazing On Stars - Selected Poems
Harry Smith
Little Things
Up North (with Eric Greinke)
t. kilgore splake
Ghost Dancer's Dreams
Splake Fishing In America
Beyond The Ghosts
Winter River Flowing - Selected Poems 1979 - 2014

Alison Stone
Dangerous Enough
Lloyd Van Brunt
Delirium - Selected Poems
Marine Robert Warden
Beyond The Straits
A. D. Winans
The Other Side Of Broadway - Selected Poems 1965-2006
Wind On His Wings
This Land Is Not My Land
Leslie H. Whitten Jr.
The Rebel - Poems By Charles Baudelaire

For information about these and other titles, please visit our website www.presapress.com.

Available through Baker & Taylor, The Book House, Coutts Information Services, Midwest Library Services, local bookstores & directly from the publisher.

Exclusive European distribution through Gazelle Book Service Ltd.
White Cross Mills, Hightown, Lancaster, LA1 4XS, UK
sales@gazellebooks.co.uk www.gazellebooks.co.uk